T0316248

SISTERS
SUCH DEVOTED SISTERS

Russell Barr

SISTERS
SUCH DEVOTED SISTERS

OBERON BOOKS
LONDON

First published in 2005 by Oberon Books Ltd
521 Caledonian Road, London N7 9RH
Tel: 020 7607 3637 / Fax: 020 7607 3629
e-mail: oberon.books@btconnect.com
www.oberonbooks.com

A catalogue record for this book is available from the British Library.

ISBN: 1 84002 567 0

Cover photo: Chris Nash

This play is dedicated to the memory of Fritha Goodey.
A great actress, and my friend.

The author wishes to thank the following for their continued support: Lois Keidon and Daniel Brine at the Live Arts Development Board, Yve Newbold, Gareth James, Joanna Scanlan, Mark Ravenhill, Alan Ayckbourn, Aileen Sherry, Chris Hay, Ruth Young, Heloise Gillingham, St John Donald, Alice Dunne, Damien Stirk, MAC Cosmetics and all the super individuals at Out of Joint.

Special thanks to Max Stafford-Clark.

Character

BERNICE

This version of *Sisters Such Devoted Sisters* was first presented at the Traverse Theatre, Edinburgh by Out of Joint on 5 August 2004. The Associate Director for Out of Joint was Naomi Jones. The original cast was as follows:

BERNICE, Russell Barr

The play won the inaugural Carol Tambor Award for the Best Production at the Edinburgh Festival 2004.

Sisters Such Devoted Sisters

As the audience enters a dark space they are surrounded by the brutal sound of people fighting, deafening traffic and dogs barking. BERNICE is stood behind a gold curtain. After a while, BERNICE enters, pours herself some tea with lemon, and begins to drink.

The noise abates.

Lights up on BERNICE.

BERNICE

I was in drag, in the back of a Halal butcher's meat truck. There were two other drag queens who were also in the truck. I, however, was buried in offal; in kidneys and livers and sweetbreads and pigs' trotters. I remember when I used to go and visit my granny – she'd be gnawing on a boiled pig's trotter as she was watching the television. There would be a little pile of them by the side of her. I think that was in between her setting fire to herself.

At the back of the truck were meat hooks. And on the hooks were pig and cow carcasses. I don't know who was driving the truck but they were driving very fast. Maybe they were drunk. And I remember we swerved round a corner and one of the cow carcasses knocked over one of the drag queens and there was great hilarity. The drag queens were having a bit of a 'kerry-on', you know, lobbing bits of old kidney at each other. One of the drag queens leant down and he picked up a pig's heart, and he opened it up and he pulled out the aorta and he slapped the other drag queen across the face with it. Behaving a bit like little boys trying to scare little girls. And I remember when I was a little boy, I would often be found at the rugby club, stealing birds' nests and ripping the heads off baby chicks, and stamping on frogs and putting them in my sister's Coke.

When I was very small I was allowed inside the rugby club, and I spent most of my time sat on my Auntie Norah's lap, dipping her pearls into her Guinness and then sucking the pearls dry.

I was a great one for playing in puddles full of glass, and one Saturday afternoon I cut off half my thumb, and I have no feeling in that part of my finger at all –

BERNICE shows her thumb to the audience.

– in fact you could put a knife through it and I would feel nothing…

My best friend, when I was at school, was a boy called Alan Strong. When Alan first met my mother he said, 'Is that Old Dutch your mother?'

And my mother never liked him after that because she said he had no manners. And Alan wanted to be a DJ when he grew up but he only had one record, which was *Three Wheels On My Wagon.* I remember I had arranged to kiss my first girlfriend. Her name was Hazel Anderson. I had planned it two weeks in advance – apparently that's what you did in Glasgow before you kissed your first girl. And we were all there and Alan was playing *Three Wheels On My Wagon* and I was snogging Hazel Anderson, and she pulled away from me and she said, 'Oh Russell,' she said, 'you're a really crap kisser!'

And I said to her, 'Well you smell. Have you got your period?'

Me and Alan used to do this thing where we would get Mother's Pride white bread and put baking powder on it, and put it out into his back garden. And pigeons would fly down and they would take the Mother's Pride bread and they'd carry it off. And what happens when pigeons eat baking-powder on white bread is that their stomachs begin to expand, and then they explode. We used to watch a little fireworks display of exploding pigeons.

I should at this point say that at any time that I substitute the word 'puppy' – as in young dog – for somebody's name, it means I am not allowed to use that person's name for legal reasons...

I would go on holiday when I was a boy to an island off the West Coast of Scotland called Arran. You would have to get a boat there. It would take about forty-five minutes. We would go and visit my Auntie Puppy and Uncle Puppy.

And we would save up my pocket-money and buy paracetamols... Actually I don't think we saved up our pocket-money, I just think that we stole them out the medicine cabinet. And we'd buy scones from the canteen. And we'd put paracetamol on a bit of scone and hold it out to the side of the boat. Seagulls would fly in and take the paracetamol and the scone and they'd carry it off. And you get a much better explosion with a paracetamol.

My Auntie Puppy and Uncle Puppy – their mummy was called Mrs Puppy; we were never allowed to know her first name – and Auntie Puppy and Uncle Puppy and Mrs Puppy had twelve Jack Russells. And in their house at home they had a bay window. And Mrs Puppy had a little automatic Mini that sat facing the bay window. One day Uncle Puppy decided that we would take all the dogs for a walk up to Brodick Castle. So he put all the Jack Russells into the Mini and started the engine up. Then Uncle Puppy realised he had left something in the house so he went away back in and one of the dogs put the car into 'drive' and another dog put its foot on the accelerator and the whole car came shooting through the front of the house past Mrs Puppy in her therapeutic chair with all the Jack Russells on the dashboard –

(*She makes a barking sound.*) 'Aye-ya-ya! Aye-ya-ya! Aye-ya-ya!'

And Mrs Puppy said, 'For goodness' sake! Really and truly Puppy, the dogs have just driven through the front of the house!'

Auntie Puppy is trying to sue me for telling that story, but she owes the council tax thirty-five thousand pounds, so I'm not sure she's going to get very far. Also Uncle Puppy is still claiming Mrs Puppy's pension, and Mrs Puppy has been dead for four years.

The back of the Halal truck was open. It had one of those rusty shutter doors, and through the offal I could see these very beautiful glass cages filled with dogs: Dobermans, Alsatians, and Rottweilers. Rabid dogs. Dogs that looked as though they were going to kill a child. And there was a biblical swarm of dragonflies. The pavement was lined with men with plastic hair. And the dragonflies would fly in and land on the men's shoulders and at that point the men's hearts would explode.

And you couldn't see any tarmac on the road. All you could see were squirrels that had been squashed by cars with their eyes popped out.

By this point the drag queens had become very aggressive and I remember they started to kick the offal on top of me and I remember there was so much of it on me that I wasn't able to breathe any more.

Long pause.

There had been a spate of… I'm not sure that 'spate' is a word…is it? Anyway, there had been a series of murders and rapes in Glasgow and one particular night four women had been raped and killed and dumped outside Washington Street, which is a disused primary school in Glasgow. And the next day I was on my way to work – I worked in a drag bar then called Madame Gillespie's – and I was walking past the scene of the crime and it had all that 'DO NOT CROSS' tape. And I was stopped by a police lady and she said to me, 'Where were you last night?'

And I said, 'I was at my work.'

She said, 'Do you know what happened here?'

And I said, 'No.'

'Four women were raped and killed.'

And I think at the time I thought, 'Oh lucky them.'

She said, 'Where do you work?'

I said, 'Madame Gillespie's'

And she went, 'Oh that's that tranny bar, isn't it?'

And I went, 'Well, no, it's not a tranny bar, it's for drag queens.'

She said, 'Do you wear women's clothes?'

I said, 'Uh huh.'

She said, 'Well, I don't think you're going to be much of a fucking suspect then are you? You can just bugger off.'

And I went on my way to Gillespie's.

Gillespie's was situated underneath the M8 flyover in Glasgow. On a street called Cheapside Street – appropriately named. And it was a disused snooker hall that they had turned into a nightclub. And it had a Roman theme: I've got no idea why it was called Madame Gillespie's. I think it's shut down now and half of it is a Chinese restaurant and the other half is a children's nursery.

And when you went in the club there were all these polystyrene statues of men with togas on with very big bulges, and it had Emperor Nero wallpaper, with his head printed hundreds of times across the wall. And above the bar it said 'BIGUS DIKUS' in luminous lights.

And the men's toilets were called 'Centurions' and the ladies toilets were called 'Centuriesses'. And because I was a lady I always use the 'Centuriesses' toilet. And I was in there one night – I was in applying my lipstick – and these two girls come in, and they go in a cubicle either side of each other. And they starts talkin' to themselves over the wall of the cubicle and one of them says, 'How are you gettin' on with the preparation for Janine's weddin'?'

And the other one says, 'Oh, we had our first fittin' for the bridesmaids' dresses and they're lovely. You should see the taffeta she's chosen…'

'But the wedding's not for two and a half years.'

'Uh-huh, but you've got to plan these things in advance. Things get really booked up.'

'Has she decided on the posy yet?'

'Oh. Uh-huh, we've found these lovely dyed green carnations – they're really gorgeous.'

'So, what colour is the taffeta?'

And the other one says,

Bernice grips the side of the chair as if on the toilet forcing something out.

'Neighh-vee bluhh!'

We were there for rehearsals that day. We did lip-synching shows. We did a 'Boogie

Boogie Bugilee Boy', and we did a 'Vogue', you know, Madonna's 'Vogue'? I've got a photograph of us here doing the Madonna routine.

And we wore the big crinoline dresses, and big wigs, you know.

But there was nobody in the club that day, except Diborah and Sadie the cleaning ladies – Diborah being the Glaswegian version of Deborah – and they were your typical sort of cleaners, you know, they wore green gingham house-coats, never afraid to get their hands down dirty toilets or dirty sinks. I remember my granny had one of those gingham house-coats and she was able to put her hand on a boiling hot frying-pan and never feel any pain.

Diborah and Sadie were usually a cheery pair, and that day they looked really miserable. And I went over to the table and I said, 'Oh Sadie,' I said, 'you look terrible.'

And Diborah said, 'Oh son,' she said, 'the most terrible thing happened to Sadie last night.'

And I said… 'What is it?'

And Diborah nudged Sadie and said, 'Go on, tell the boy whit happened.'

And there was a pause… 'I goes up to the front door last night and I puts the key in the door and the door's already open. And I goes intae ma front room and I've been fuckin' burgled. They've stolen evrithin. They may has well have got a fuckin' Pickford's van rune. An' they've even stolen ma "hoo-er's knickers".'

For those of you that don't know, that's Glaswegian slang for 'Austrian Blinds'.

'An' you won't believe this son. But I've been fuckin' scoofed.'

And 'scoofed' means they steal the radiators and the pipes. Can you believe Glasgow's got a word for that?

'An' I goes away intae the kitchen and those dirty, dirty, dirty burglars have shat in my vat o' soup an' I had to throw half of it away.'

I says, 'Sadie, you only threw half the soup away?'

'Well, it was a good pot. I just scooped the jobbie out and put it in the bin.'

I remember another time I went in, and I said, 'Hello Sadie, how are you?'

'I've been up the doctor's today.'

I said, 'Oh really.'

'I'm having terrible trouble with these incontinence pants, they don't fit me properly. And I go away up the doctor's and I don't have an appointment. And I've been waitin' about two hours and I nudge the lady next to me and I say, "Gonna get one of those nurses over, I'm having terrible trouble with these pants."'

'So the nurse comes over and says, "Can I help you, dear?"'

'"Uh huh, you've prescribed me the wrong pants, I'm having to wear my husband's trousers, tie them up with a big bit of rope…"'

'And the nurse says, "Well, if you wouldn't mind just showing me a pair of the pants."'

So Sadie stands up and pulls down her husband's trousers.

And the nurse says, 'Those are for your bed. Those aren't for wearing.'

She had got the mattress and tied it up like a big nappy.

After a while the other boys arrived. There was a group of us that used to hang about at Gillespie's. I've got a photograph of us here.

Shows audience photograph.

There was me, and…

Shows other photograph.

…my name was Bernice Hindley – Myra Hindley's niece – 'cause we thought that my wig looked a bit like Myra Hindley's wig. Not that Myra wore a wig, but anyway. And I had a bingo evening on a Monday called 'Bernice's Barmy Bingo'. And I'd go in each Monday and there would be a grey envelope on my dressing-room table and I would open it up and it would say 'Holloway Prison' at the top and it would say 'My Darling Niece' and there would be all this stuff about identifying bits of children's arms and a bit of kiddy porn and a bit about her lesbian affair. And at the bottom it would say 'from your loving Auntie Myra'.

And then there was Gerry – or Geraldine, as his name was in drag, imaginatively enough. And Gerry, I think, was addicted to speed and sun-shimmer in the same quantities – I don't think he had ever seen a sunbed. Eh, Glasgow has more tanning salons per person than anywhere else in Great Britain. He looks a bit there like a Pakistani lady…

Shows photograph.

…but is in fact white underneath all the makeup.

Gerry was also partial to a bit of GHB which is Rohypnol the date-rape drug – GBH, I used to call it. And he would freeze it in his freezer and then heat it up in the microwave before he took it. Why you would take the date-rape drug recreationally is beyond me.

And then there was Darren – or Doris, as his name was in drag. And people thought Doris a particularly nasty individual. I always thought he was rather nice. The first night he was at Gillespie's he spent the whole night being fucked in the disabled toilet. And Doris had a karaoke evening on a Thursday called 'Doris's Karaoke'. And he had all the computer, the screen and everything. And he had two pedals at his feet: one for the smoke machine and one for the reverb. And I remember one night he got all the pedals mixed up and the smoke machine blew up and he had to go into hospital for carbon monoxide poisoning.

And then there was this boy here.

Points to photograph.

I don't really know much about him. He was the boyfriend of Robert, who was the manager of the club, who's now in prison for embezzlement. But he was rather insignificant; I don't really remember much about him.

We came into the club one day and there was the most terrible smell of burning plastic and we couldn't figure out where the smell was coming from, and then we heard this god-almighty scream coming from the dressing-room and Doris comes out holding this flaming wig that somebody's left too close to one of the bulbs. He was furious 'cause he'd saved up all his money from the cruise ships to buy the wig. And Gerry said, 'Uch, I don't mind,' he said, 'I'll wear that wig.'

So Gerry used to kick about with a wig with a big burnt hole in it.

And then there was Ross...

Pause.

... And I...

Pause.

...fell in love with Ross. Ross was an extraordinary mixture: one minute he'd be holding your hand while he was talking to you and the next minute he'd be punching you in the face. And he had three scars down the right-hand side of his cheek and two false teeth on a plate that he used to click in and out. His boyfriend Paul had no teeth at all, which Ross said was very good for blowjobs. I don't fancy trying it myself. And Ross and Paul had a very violent relationship. And I remember going round their house one day and there was a hole through the kitchen door. And I said, 'What happened there?'

And Ross said, 'Uch, I put Paul's head through it last night.'

We used to go flyering at Gillespie's, round the bars. And I met up with Ross one night and he was carrying this big metal scaffolding pole, and I said to him, 'What are you going to do with that?' And Ross sais, 'Uch, I'm going to hit Paul with it later on...

And Ross had lent me once a pair of 'Ver-Snatchie' underpants – that's what we call Versace in Glasgow. The only place that has a 'Ver-Snatchie' shop, apart from London, is Glasgow. And Paul had given Ross these 'Ver-Snatchie' pants as a five-year wedding anniversary present. And I had lost the pants… Well, I hadn't lost them. I'd left them with big skit stains down the inside that I couldn't wash out and I had to hide them behind the wardrobe.

And the next day Ross came in and he had two black eyes for losing the pants.

And then there were the punters, you know, the people, that used to come to the club. There was Laura Sloan and Laura was a professional shoplifter. And I think she influenced my shoplifting career of later years: I stole sixty thousand pounds' worth of clothes from the Gap. And you know 'Autograph'? – that posh Marks & Spencer's range? Well, they may as well've had a big sign outside saying, 'Please come in here and help yourself – everything free today.' I cleared seven suede coats at five hundred pounds a go in one lot. And I worked in a, eh, Young Offenders' Unit, you know, for naughty kids. And I would steal at the weekends and then sell the stuff to the staff during the week.

Laura's sister Lily was also a professional shoplifter and Laura and Lily's mother used to crack safes in banks. But she had become a bit incontinent because of the drink. She had a little scrapbook of all the banks that she had cracked. And I remember going round to their house one day and Laura was shoving her mother down the front stairs,

'Get out ma hoose you pishy auld cow. Pish in my new leather sofa – you're a dirty, fucking cunt and don't come back.'

And sure enough you went in and there was a little pool of yellow wee on the leather sofa.

Laura was barred from Buchanan Street in Glasgow. If she was ever spotted on that street she would be immediately arrested. And I remember we were in 'Ver-Snatchie' one day and she was trying on a pair of eight-thousand-pound, diamond and ruby encrusted shoes. And while they was trying the shoes on she stole eight pairs of sunglasses out the window. She would always steal me a wee tin of Blue Jeans aftershave which I always thought was very sweet of her.

Pause.

She stole a Yorkshire Terrier from a party once because she said, 'the lady wasn't looking after it properly.' And the next day had no recollection of it and pulled back the covers and there was this Yorkshire Terrier looking at her from the bottom of the bed. She eventually got put in prison for stealing a pair of socks form The Sock Shop and she told her kids she'd gone to Marbella for nine months.

Then there was Willie Johnson. And Willie Johnson used to batter credit cards, which means he had about fifty stolen credit cards. We would always get stuff out shops or fill my mother's car up with petrol using the cards. And he became very friendly with a very famous Celtic footballer, Puppy Mac A Puppy, and they set up a little cocaine business in Glasgow. I think they've now got a hotel which is just the front of a hotel with the coke business that's going on behind. And Willie also had a very violent relationship with his boyfriend. And I remember Willie used to tell me, 'I fuck that fucking cunt of a boyfriend of mine until he fucking bleeds.'

Long pause.

When my mum and dad got married my mum was with her father waiting for the cars to come round. And the booking company had got the cars mixed up and they sent hearses instead of wedding cars. So my mum and her dad had to cram in beside the driver, you know, with the space for the coffin in the back, and off they went to the church.

And I'm from a very middle-class family. My grandfather was the Mayor of Motherwell but a chronic alcoholic. And mum said that after he died they cleared out his office and they pulled back each law book and there was a bottle of vodka behind each one.

If you look up the Alcoholics' Anonymous handbook you can see where all the meetings are all over the country. And Sheffield's got thirty-eight A.A. meetings and Manchester's got fifty-eight A.A. meetings and Glasgow's got four hundred and eighty-seven A.A. meetings You can go at any time of the day or night.

Pause.

My Nan was always trying to commit suicide because of her husband's drinking, and mum would say they'd go home once a month and Nan would be stood on the top of the house with the fire brigade there, ready to throw herself off. But she never would – she'd just climb back in the window and then go to her bed for a month until she did it again and everyone would fend for themselves.

They had a pet Minor bird when they were children called Jean and every time somebody walked through the door Jean would shout, 'Cunt! Cunt! You're a cunt!'

So they had to have the Minor bird put down in the end…

And when Nan became very old she became very, very, very fat and the doctor said, 'You're gonna have to put her on a diet or summin' 'cause she's gonna kill herself.'

So we put her on the 'SlimFast Plan'. And I went in one day an' she had a bowl of meringues and she was dipping the meringues into the SlimFast. And she had done fifty years lifeboat service for the R.N.L.I. and she was invited down to the Royal Festival Hall to meet the, eh, the Princess of, the Duchess of Kent. Uch, I canny remember what she's called, you know the one that's always at Wimbledon with the white hair. She got invited in to meet her and she got a new outfit and off she went to the Festival Hall. And she's waiting in the audience for her name to come up. And as she goes up for the award she trips over a Hoover cable and they canny get her back up. Mind you the doctor had told us you'd need a fork-lift truck to get her back up. So sadly she never got to meet the 'Tennis Duchess' in the end.

She had three duaghters, and her middle daughter, Alison, had multiple sclerosis and cancer. Never a very good combination. And she was married to Uncle Kenneth who was a member of the Orangemen's Lodge in Glasgow – basically a Nazi. He got an electronic Christmas card every year and you would open it up and it would be Santa Claus dressed as an Orangeman singing 'The Sash'.

We would go on holiday to North Berwick and I remember at breakfast one day he nudged me and he said, 'See her?'

'See who?'

'See the waitress? She's one.'

And I said, 'She's what?'

'She's a Catholic.'

I said, 'How can you tell?'

'You can tell by their kneecaps.'

You know, from all the praying.

Uncle Kenneth keeps Quality Street tins filled with one pound coins buried in his back garden. He's got three thousands pounds scattered all over his garden. So if any of you are ever a bit short, he lives at fifty-six Roddinghead Road, Newton Mearns, Glasgow.

When Uncle Kenneth, Auntie Ally, Uncle Kenneth, no... Auntie Ally had become very, very sick and she had lost all her hair so she had to wear a wig. She was put in a hospital called the 'Bon Secour', which was run by nuns. As you can imagine that went down really well with Uncle Kenneth. And after she had died the nun came out of the room and said, (*Adopts accent.*) 'I'm sorry to say that Auntie Ally has passed away.'

She was from the Highlands of Scotland.

'So we're just going to make her look nice for you.'

I sound Welsh, don't I? I don't sound like I'm form the highlands at all. She'll have to be Welsh for this story.

'So, we're just going to make her look nice for you. If you wouldn't mind just stepping out the room for a minute.'

So we all left the room and waited ten minutes and then the nun came back in the room, and she said,

'Okay, Auntie Ally's ready to be viewed now.'

So we went in and the nun had put Auntie Ally's wig on back to front with the label sticking out of the front.

And the nun said, 'Now, you're going to have to get the rings off, you know. Because when people die their hands swell up. So you're going to have to get the engagement ring and the wedding ring off.'

So mum said she was saying that she was pulling at Auntie Ally's hands but the more she pulled the hand and the more the wig went squinter and squinter. Mum said she laughed so much she nearly wet herself.

Pause.

My grandfather on my father's side was addicted to gambling so they lived in a house that had no electricity and no hot water.

My granny always recommended whisky for everything. Anything that was ever wrong with you, whisky was the answer. And I suffered from very bad earache when I was a boy and I woke up in the middle of the night with the most terrible pain in my ear and granny came in and went, 'I've got just the thing for that.' She went away into the kitchen and you could hear her boiling up whisky in the frying pan. She'd pour it into a little jug and then pour boiling hot whisky into your ear.

When Granny had got old, she'd had two strokes, so she was put in a residential home. She was always getting in terrible trouble with cigarettes. We got a phone call from the fire brigade one day to say that she'd set the flat on fire and they couldn't find her and could we come down. So we all goes down to the residential home. And the fire brigade were there and my mother was crying. And the smoke was billowing out and all you could see was the burnt cuckoo-clock on the side of the wall. And then after a while through the smoke I could see this Zimmer frame moving along the corridor. Nobody pushing it. Like a poltergeist Zimmer frame. Moving of its own accord. And after a while Granny appeared through the smoke looking like one of the black and white minstrels, you know, with the black face and singed hair and a big hole in her nightie. And she says to me, 'Ah-right son? How are you?' like nothing had happened.

She was eventually put in a proper nursing home and she sat beside a lady who would keep a carving-knife down her stockings.

My grandfather was also addicted to porn. But not your mainstream porn, like *Fiesta* or *Playboy*, but stuff to do with small children.

Long pause.

In the *Daily Record*, in Glasgow, it said that a mother had named her newborn child 'Pocahontas McBride'. Imagine what a torturin' she was gonna get when she was older: 'Ah-right wee Pokey?'

Long pause.

My mother has a slight addiction to Benilyn cough syrup, and she plays a lot of golf. So she was driving back from her golf one day along the motorway and she saw a microwave oven in the lay-by and she thought, 'Oh super,' you know, 'something to defrost my butter in.' So she pulled in, puts the microwave in the back of the car and she drove off. An' the police starts to follow her and they're flashing their lights and she's thinking, 'I'm not doing anything wrong.' So they flash their lights a bit more and she pulls in. The police car pulls in behind and knocks on the window and says, 'If you wouldn't mind just stepping out the car, madam.'

And my mother says, 'Uh-huh. Sure. No problem officer.'

And the police officer says, 'You've just stolen our speed-check monitor from the side of the road.'

Pause.

My mother hangs around with a whole load of girls on a Saturday afternoon: they all sit about drinkin' gin – they're all my adopted aunties – and I was with them one day and Auntie Rosie was there, and she says to me, 'Have you heard of that toy shop, The Jolly Giant?'

I says, 'Uh huh.'

She said, 'Well, they have opened up a new one.'

'Oh have they really?'

'Uh huh, it's called Tossers Toy Shop.'

'Tossers Toy Shop?'

She said, 'Have you never heard of it?'

I says, 'No.'

She said, 'I'm surprised you've never heard of it, there is a big chain of them all over the country.'

I said 'Rosie, how do you spell that?'

'T – O – Y– S – R – U – S.'

I said, 'That's Toys 'R' Us…!'

Ross had wanted me to take an ekky. I'd never taken an Ecstasy before. And we were all at Gillespie's and me and Gerry and Ross got off early and we were all in drag and we went off the Club X, which is one of the gay clubs in Glasgow. And we took an ekky but it must've been a paracetamol as it had no effect whatsoever. So Ross says, 'I know somewhere where we can get a really good ekky.'

So we all got in my mother's car – she had a red, little Nissan Micra called 'Colette'. And we all got in that. And we drove to Easterhouse in drag. Now Easterhouse is a very, very rough council estate in Glasgow. So we were driving through the estate and Ross points to one of the flats and says, 'Ma dad murdered somebody in that block of flats. Stabbed them in the face.'

And I remember trying to question Ross on it and he wouldn't say anymore about it. So we gets up to the block of flats where we're getting the ekkys and Ross says to me, 'Right, this is a guy who I used to go out with and his name's Tommy and he's an insomniac, he hasn't slept for five and a half years and he's got a very aggressive bulldog.'

And I said, 'Right. Okay.' And we all got out the car.

And we go up the close, you know, past all the pishy nappies.

Gerry used to do this thing where he would rub his crotch and waggle his tongue at the same time and shout, 'Right!' I've got no idea why he did it. So as we're going up the stairs Gerry's shouting, 'Right!' and we gets to the front door and we knock the door and Tommy answers the door. And sure enough it's like something out of *Night of the Living Dead*, with the aggressive bulldog beside him.

The audience hear the noise of a tap dripping.

And we go into the flat and out the corner of my eye I can see the bath filled with black, stagnant bathwater. And we goes into the living room and everything's black: the walls, the carpet, the coffee-table. And on the coffee-table were about twenty ekkys all laid out in rows. And Ross used to have to take about eight ekkys to get a hit off it and Gerry about four and they said I should just take a half since I'd never had one before. And Ross said the sign of a good ekky is as it's going through your system you go and have an ekky shite. So we all went off and out jobbies and we came back into the room. And I remember loving the way the ekky made me feel; it made the skin on my arms go 'kkuhhh' and we told funny stories and we did the Madonna routine in the front room, you know, and Gerry did quite a lot of shouting of 'Right!'

And Tommy wasn't taking any ekkys; he was taking something in a brown prescription bottle. And I says to him, 'What are those for?'

And he said, 'Oh, they're for Parkinson's Disease.'

I said, 'Have you got Parkinson's Disease?'

He said, 'Naww. I just like the way they make me feel.'

Time went so quickly and before we knew it was ten o'clock in the morning and the ice-cream van was coming round – I remember it played the *Ghostbusters'* theme tune – and we all thought we'd go down for a wee 'ninty-nine' cone. Still in drag. And we're in the queue with the kids waiting for our cones and out the side of my eye I can see an old lady in a wheelchair selling 'jellies', or temazepams, to kids for a fiver a go. And one of the boys comes up and he pushed the old lady over in the wheelchair and she came rolling out.

The first and only time I took a temazepam I lost four days.

Pause.

Mind you it wasn't like the time I took an acid and got lost in the cubicle of McDonald's for five and a half hours because I couldn't find the door, but that's another story.

Long pause.

We have a spiral staircase in our house at home. And I was about five – I have very little memory of being a child – and I climbed the stair and I went into one of the cupboards and the cupboard was filled with brown leather briefcases, with my father's initials R.M.B. on them.

My dad's had loads of different jobs: he worked for Rosetta Fruit Juices, and he fitted mirrored wardrobes and he also had a mushroom growing factory that he operated out of the garage at the back of our house. And he lined the walls of the garage with bin-bags, you know, to keep the moisture in. And Tesco's rang him one day and said could he supply four hundred and fifty punnets a week and he said, 'Yes.' Out the garage!

The leather briefcases were filled with pornographic magazines – but your mainstream porn, like *Fiesta / Playboy*. There was a bit of Swedish porn in there as well. And Alistair White would come from across the road, he lived at number twenty, and he was about three. And my sister Alison – she was also three. And me and Alistair would be naked except for my nan's mink coats and my sister would just be wearing my mother's wedding veil. And we'd get the *Fiesta* magazines and we'd spread them over the carpet so's you couldn't see any carpet. I remember my favourite page in *Fiesta* was the readers' page – you know, Polaroids of them stood in their front room. And me and Alistair – I remember being very sexually excited – and we would both get my sister and pin her up against the wall. And we'd spread her legs. And we would both put our hands up my sister.

Gesture of hand going up.

Pause.

The porn became like my trophies, you know. I loved showing them off to people, and David Scott, who was my best friend, he lived on the same side of the road as us and he came down one day and we cut out all the bosoms and fannys out the *Fiesta* magazine and put them on a big bit of card, you know, like a big collage and showed them to my mother. As you can imagine, she was thrilled. And I remember the next day seeing my father leaving, carrying all the leather briefcases.

Pause.

Apparently, outside one of the clinics in Los Angeles there was a billboard that said, 'Book your Caesarean here and keep your passages honeymoon fresh.'

Pause.

I prostituted myself twice while I was at Gillespie's. The first night, me, Gerry, Ross got off work early and we goes up to Blythswood Square which is where all the prostitutes hang about in Glasgow. And we were stood at this prostitute's patch and she comes over and says, 'Listen, the tranny patch is down the road.'

Anyway, we got talking to her and she had a bit of vodka in her handbag and she wouldn't give any of the vodka to Ross, so Ross punched her in the face and the pimp comes along so we cleared off. So we're walking down the hill and then Ross gets picked up by a black taxi driver – well, the taxi was black, the driver wasn't, if you see what I mean – and they all went off to Strathclyde Park or wherever you go if you get picked up by a taxi driver. An' me an' Gerry weren't having any luck so we just thought we'd go back to Gillespie's. And as we were walking back there were these two bus drivers coming towards us. One of them very young and attractive and the other one very old and not attractive at all, and of course I get the old one.

The difference between me and Gerry and Ross is that Gerry and Ross looked like ladies, of a kind, and I just looked like a big drag-queen; you know, in a big, sort of see-through, turquoise nightie and ruby slippers, you know.

So, I'm talking away to the old guy and he says to me, 'Do you wanta come up the bus station?'

And you thought, 'Well, there's an offer you can't refuse.'

So me and Gerry goes off to Anderson Bus Station. And Gerry got on the number forty-four to Carnwardric and I got on the number thirty-seven to Govan. So I'm sat on the disabled seat on the bus with the old guy beside me. And through the window I can see Gerry with his face squashed up against the door of the bus being fucked by the driver, with all that false tan, you know, smeared all over the inside. So the old guy stars rubbing himself and he says, 'Come on…'

And I says, 'What?'

And he pulls down his trousers. And the smell. And I remember I couldn't do anything. I just remember asking him what route he took to Govan.

The second time it was Halloween, and I had finished work and I was walking home – I lived in a flat that my dad had bought me on the south side of Glasgow. And I was walking past Bennet's – which is one of the other gay clubs in Glasgow – an' I gets stopped by a friend of mine. And he says to me, 'Listen, there's this guy over there who wants someone to dress up for him and he'll pay ye.'

And I says, 'What does he look like?'

So he points over at this very beautiful six-foot-five guy. And I says, 'Okay. He can come back as long as he pays for the taxi an' he pays me.'

So we get in the taxi. And we don't talk. And we goes up the close into the flat. An' I says to him, 'Right, you go in the bedroom, I'll be about an hour getting ready.'

And I thought, 'Well I'd better look attractive,' you know, so I had a little BHS bra and panties set and a little lacy kimono. And I goes into the bedroom and he's lying on the bed wanking himself off and he pulls me towards him and he starts to kiss me. There's nothing more unattractive than seeing a man with that pink lipstick, you know, smeared all over his mouth. And he gets my panty-girdle and he yanks it down. And he gives me a blowjob and then I do the same to him. And then he says to me, 'I want you to fuck me.'

'You want *me* to fuck *you*?'

And he went, 'Uh-huh.'

'Have you ever been fucked before?'

And he went, 'No.'

And I went, 'Right.'

I find fucking a bit of a palaver really, you know, with the packets, the poppers an' everthin' else. So I get all the stuff out the sock drawer and I take it up to the bed. And I'm trying to undo the packets and the nails are falling off and it was a disaster and everything went limp and he went off to the toilet.

And his wallet was lying on the floor – I would often steal from people that I slept with. Ross taught me how… Well, not that it takes much teaching. You just lift the wallet and take the money out. It's quite straightforward – so, I lent over the bed and flipped his wallet open and he was the Chief Inspector of the fraud squad in Glasgow. It didn't faze me really and he comes back in the room, and I said, 'What do you do for a living?'

He says, 'I'm a policeman.'

I says, 'Are you married?'

He says, 'Uh-huh.'

'Have you got kids?'

He goes, 'Aye.' He says to me, 'I want to sleep with you with all the gear on.'

I said, 'Oh fuck off. I'll never get any sleep.'

So I gave him my telephone number. He
phoned for several days after that but I
didn't answer the phone.

Pause.

He gave me twenty quid.

Pause.

Me and Ross thought, for a wee change,
we'd go through to Edinburgh for a night
out. And we went to the, the gay club – I
canny remember what the gay club's called
in Edinburgh…Bum…Brumbles?
Bum…Bobbles? Bozzlies? Bozzells we'll
have to call it, I can't remember what it's
called – so we all got into Colette – me and
Ross – and drove off to Bozzells. Now, we
weren't taking any drugs that day. We were
taking this body-builder, you know, a steroid
powder – and you're only supposed to take
half a teaspoon and we'd taken seven
tablespoons of this powder – which they also
test out on mice. So we were wired to the
moon on this mice powder. And I don't
remember anything about being in Bozzells
at all except we meet these guys from
Dundee – who invite us back to a party.

Now, to drive from Edinburgh to Dundee's really far. It takes about three hours, or as far as I can remember it took three hours.

So I says to Ross, 'Come on, let's go.' I was up for anything from the mice powder, you know.

And Ross said, 'Oh, I don't think we should go.'

And I said, 'Why not?'

He says, ''Cause if I don't get back for Paul he'll fuckin' kill me.'

I says, 'Oh. Let's not go then.'

Pause.

And Ross says, 'Oh let's just go anyway.'

So we get in the car. And we drove through. And I don't remember anything about being at the party at all.

And the next morning we were driving back. Ross would always drive my mother's car. I was never allowed to drive it and didn't have a driving licence. So we were driving back an' I takes an asthma attack in the car and I don't have my puffer with me. So I starts to be sick out the window of the car and there's blood in the sick and Ross says, 'For fuck's sake, would you quit doin' that. I've got to get back to Paul. He's gonna fuckin' do me in.'

And then the car breaks down. So we're at the side of the road and the passenger door's open an' I'm throwing up the blood. And Ross says to me, 'Just get out the fuckin' car and get up to the fuckin' SOS phone and get us the fuck out a here.'

So I walk up, throwin' up the blood, and I get to the orange box and open it up and pick up the phone. And there's a voice that goes, 'Hello-hello?'

An' he can hear me being sick. An' he says, 'I'm phoning an ambulance.'

I say, 'Don't.'

He says, 'I'm phoning an ambulance.'

So I don't make it back to the car and the ambulance picks me up and they give me an oxygen mask and they give me a shot of steroids – not that I needed any more after all that mice powder.

And we get back to the car – there was nothing wrong with the car, we'd just run out of petrol. And, and I can hear Ross shouting, 'Get him out the fuckin' back o' that ambulance. There's nothing wrong with him. He's only doing that for attention.'

Anyway, we go off to the hospital and I tell the nurse what's happened. So when Ross comes to pick me up the nurse says, 'I want a word wi' you. You canny just leave people when they've got asthma. It's a serious business.'

And Ross goes to punch the female nurse and I stand in the way and Ross goes off to the car park and I go after him. And then Ross punches me in the face and I fall to the floor unconscious and I come to and he says, 'Get in the car.'

BERNICE shakes her head.

'Get in the car or I'll fuckin' kill you.'

So I get in the car. And we drive back to
Glasgow, him chain-smoking B&H the
whole way home, very good for the asthma.

And I was wearing a pair of his 'Ver-
Snatchie' trousers that he had lent me…
Ross lived right in the centre of Glasgow, on
Miller Street. And it was Saturday afternoon
by this point so it was very busy with people
shopping. And Ross says to me, 'Get out the
car.'

So I get out the car.

And he says, 'Go and stand in the middle of
the road.'

So I go over to the middle of the road.

He says to me, 'Take the trousers off.' And
he makes me take the trousers off while
everybody watches.

For three weeks after that he called my
mother every day and called her a cunt and
threatened to kill her.

Long pause.

Doris – Darren had moved into my flat in Glasgow. I had a spare room and he'd been there four months but he'd never paid any rent as he was addicted to speed. And my dad said, 'Get that bugger out of here. He's to be out by Friday. We canny have people in there that don't pay…'

Anyway, the Friday comes and I'm in my bed with…my pyjamas on 'cause I've been working the night before. And in my flat in Glasgow the doors aren't solid, they've got that, you know, that seventies leaved glass. So you can see somebody through the glass but you couldn't see who it was. And the doorbell goes…

We hear the sound of a doorbell.

…and these two guys come into the flat. And I just think they're here to help Darren move so I go back to sleep. And I'm woken up by an axe going through the leaved glass window.

Loud smashing noise.

And these two guys come into my room – I had quite a lot of religious iconography at that time. I thought it was quite retro. You know, Jesus on the Cross and Saint Sebastians and Virgin Marys – and they took the Jesus off the Cross and the head off the Virgin Mary. And they came up to me in the bed and they rested the blade of their axe on my neck.

Pause.

They said, 'If we ever see you in Glasgow again we'll fuckin' kill ye. Yer a nasty wee cunt. And don't think we're fuckin' jokin'.' And the axe just nipped the skin, and the blood rolled down onto my pyjamas.

And I remember looking over at Darren and Darren was smiling.

I phoned my mum and dad. I always thought my mum and dad would come and save me but they're both chronic alcoholics. I watched my father kick my mother in the face through a hotel door in Ayr.

Pause.

Later that night I had to go back to the flat to pick up some clothes. My dad decided he was goin' to come with me, you know, for protection, not that he was going to protect me. By that point he had drunk two litre-bottles of gin. My father was the only person in our area tae get a personalised Christmas card from the Victoria Wine. On the way back we were driving mother's little Nissan Micra, Colette. We had a fight in the car – I canny even remember what the fight was about – anyway, he punched me in the face while I was driving and I got out the car. It was snowing. Dad then got in the driver's seat and drove off swerving all over the fucking road. I started walking.

Within about five minutes, I had picked a guy up, a really horrible lookin' guy and I went back to his flat in Crosshill. He had one of those cheap horrible carpets that looked as though somebody had thrown up all over it. He starts to fuck me, I was face down on the puky carpet. I remember he dribbled all over my back. I don't rembember his name even; mind you, I don't remember very many people's names that I have had sex with.

I walked back home, I had a bath and I remember I pulled back, you know, my foreskin and my jap's-eye – such a lovely expression – was all covered in blood-blisters and I took my thumbnail and I burst them.

Pause.

My dad also worked for HP sauces, you know, the brown sauce. He said he was the one that came up with the idea for putting the Houses of Parliament on the front. I'm sure that can't be true. And our garage was filled with peas and beans and brown sauce that were about four months out of date. And I had an Uncle Jim, who we called Uncle Grim, and his wife Janet who we called Granite; Granite and Grim. And Grim had a terrible fear of nuclear bombs going off so he had built this nuclear bomb shelter in his back garden. And my dad said, 'I've got just the thing for you and your nuclear shelter.'

So he gave him all the peas and the beans so that when the nuclear bomb did come they'd have stuff to survive on, you know. The nuclear bomb shelter was very expensive and about six months after that the thing collapsed.

Pause.

We put money in a kitty at Gillespie's for a wee special night. And we'd bought tickets for a barn dance on a boat on the River Clyde. So we'd all got really done up. I've got a photograph of me an' Ross here.

Shows photograph.

I had my Myra Hindley wig all done up in curls, you know, and new shoes and Ross had a lovely leather stole and a big feather plumage. We looked really fabulous. And we met up with Doris and Gerry and we goes off to the barn dance on the boat. But it was shite. How we didn't know that a barn dance on a boat wasn't going to be shite anyway. So we thought we'd go to Club X instead. And we were drinking speed in Irn Bru cans because Ross said you get more of a hit from it. And while we were in Club X we just thought we'd get a wee ekky. So we went into the ladies' toilet 'cause we knew a dealer there. And while we're gettin' our ekkies this transsexual came out one of the cubicles who used to kick about the scene in Glasgow. So Gerry says, 'Oh look Rosie, there's that fuckin' manky tranny. She's got a face like a melted welly. Still got yer three-piece suite ya cunt?'

And Ross starts, 'Ma tits are better than yours and they're fuckin' rolled up socks.'

And Darren was laughing but I didn't think it was very funny. So we leaves the toilet. I think Club X is shut down now? And there was a dancefloor and then a bar and a seating area at the back.

Points.

So we goes up to the seating area with the transsexual and the transsexual's boyfriend sat beside us. So Ross starts again, 'Are you still takin' yer hormones? Have you had your fuckin' penis tucked up inside you? You're a dirty fuckin' cunt. Folk like you should be fuckin' locked up wi' yer fake fannies.'

And the boyfriend of the transsexual gets a bottle and lobs it at Ross and it just misses Ross' face. So the bouncer comes and chucks the transsexual and the transsexual's boyfriend out the club.

And then I remember watching Ross and Gerry and they got excited. They were like a pack of wild animals. And Ross gets up to leave and Gerry follows and me and Darren go after them. And I was stood on Royal Exchange Square and I could see Ross facing the transsexual on the middle of Glassford Street with Gerry on the other side of the road. So we goes up to join them. And the transsexual and Ross were just goading each other, you know, pushing each other about. And then I think the transsexual said something about Ross' boyfriend being an 'ugly wee dwarf'. And Ross had a pair of very thick, metal, platform shoes on. And he ripped one of the shoes off and he took the shoe round the side of the transsexual's face.

Pause.

And the blood and the teeth fell out the side of her mouth.

Pause.

And she fell to the floor. And Ross turned to walk away. And the transsexual gets back up and she had a very thick gold chain on. And she ripped the chain and she flipped the chain over Ross' head and she pulled it.

Pause.

And it cut all into the skin and the blood poured down the front of his dress. And then Gerry gets a bottle and takes it over the transsexual's head and she falls to the floor unconscious. And then – I remember this very clearly – Ross came to the front of the transsexual. And he spread the transsexual's legs.

Pause.

And he took the metal heel of his shoe and just dug it in over and over again. And the blood just poured out. And then Gerry came to the head of the transsexual and he took his fist and he pounded his fist into her face over and over again.

And I remember looking over at Darren and Darren was smiling. And then Ross gets up to leave and Gerry followed. And for me to join the other boys I had to walk past the transsexual's body and she was unrecognisable. And I went and joined the other boys. I didn't go back. It was then that I started to dream about being in the back of the Halal butcher's meat truck. I didn't go back and see if she needed any help.

And I'm absolutely sure that Ross and Gerry beat her to death.

Long pause.

We hear dogs barking.

Fade to blackout.

End.